to Mary
Love
From - Ken 2/28/88

IF LOVE BE LOVE

IF
LOVE
BE
LOVE

Poems & Prose
Chosen by

REX
HARRISON

W.H. ALLEN · LONDON

Printed and bound in Great Britain
by Mackays of Chatham Ltd, Kent
for the Publisher, WH Allen & Co PLC
44 Hill Street, London W1X 8LB

ISBN 0 491 02600 5

For Mercia

I dedicate this anthology to my beloved wife
from whom I have learnt the art of living
and loving at long last.

CONTENTS

Preface

I
What is Love?

II
Courtship

III
Lovers

IV
Other Kinds of Love

V
Devotion

Acknowledgements

Preface

*Love is poetry and poetry is the honey of all flowers, the
quintessence of all sciences, the mirror of wit, and the
very phrase of angels.*

Thomas Nashe

I have enormously enjoyed reading and selecting
these tender, sweet and often humorous thoughts on
love. I started out in quite a haphazard manner but
found after much searching, that I invariably came
across a simple and direct statement of love that
somehow struck a chord in my heart.

There is no philosophical conclusion or single
view of love to be read in this selection. All of these
thoughts on love though do add up to my view of the
world 'at love'. Their poems and words dwell on this
inevitably mysterious and elusive emotion which
can make us happy or sad, comical or angry, absurd
or sentimental, treacherous or loyal. So you will find
a chapter on 'Other Kinds of Love' in addition to a
wide range of thoughts on love from Yeats, Ogden
Nash, Browning, T. S. Eliot, Shakespeare, Graves,
Dorothy Parker and many others.

All of these thoughts compose a picture of the
delight the world shows in love. And that is surely as
it should be, because love is, after all, our greatest
pleasure.

Rex Harrison
May 1979

WHAT

IS

LOVE?

Duc de la Rochefoucauld

It is difficult to define love. But we may say that in the soul, it is a ruling passion; in the mind, it is a close sympathy and affinity; in the body, a wholly secret and delicate longing to possess what we love—and this after much mystery.

René Descartes

We may, it seems to me, find differences in love according to the esteem which we bear to the object loved as compared with oneself: for when we esteem the object of love less than ourselves, we have only a simple affection for it; when we esteem it equally with ourselves, that is called friendship; and when we esteem it more, the passion which we have may be called devotion.

William Shakespeare
SONNET CXVI

Let me not to the marriage of true minds
Admit impediments. Love is not love
Which alters when it alteration finds,
Or bends with the remover to remove.
O, no! it is an ever-fixed mark
That looks on tempests and is never shaken;
It is the star to every wand'ring bark,
Whose worth's unknown, although his height
  be taken.
Love's not Time's fool, though rosy lips and cheeks
Within his bending sickle's compass come;
Love alter not with his brief hours and weeks,
But bears it out even to the edge of doom.
  If this be error and upon me proved,
   I never writ, nor no man ever loved.

Robert Burton

But the symptoms of the mind in lovers are almost infinite, and so diverse, that no art can comprehend them; though they be merry sometimes, and rapt beyond themselves for joy: yet most part love is a plague, a torture, a hell, a bitter sweet passion at last. . . . Like a summer fly or sphinx's wings, or a rainbow of all colours . . . fair, foul or full of variation, though most part irksome and bad. . . .

George MacDonald

It is by loving and not by being loved that one can come nearest the soul of another; yea, where two love it is the loving of each other, and not the being loved by each other, that originates and perfects and ensures their blessedness.

Mariolle's eyes always searched among the letters for the longed-for handwriting. When he had found it, an involuntary emotion would surge up in his heart, making it throb wildly; he always took this letter first, and would dwell on the address before tearing open the envelope. What would she say? Would the word 'love' be there? She had never yet used that word without adding 'well' or 'very much'; 'I love you well' or 'I love you very much'. How thoroughly he was used to this formula that lost all power by using additional words! Can there be much or little in loving?

To love 'very much' is to love poorly: one loves—that is all—it cannot be modified or completed without being nullified. It is a short word, but it contains all: it means the body, the soul, the life, the entire being. We feel it as we feel the warmth of the blood, we breathe it as we breathe the air, we carry it in ourselves as we carry our thoughts. Nothing more exists for us. It is not a word; it is an inexpressible state indicated by four letters. . . .

e e cummings

love is more thicker than forget
more thinner than recall
more seldom than a wave is wet
more frequent than to fail

it is most mad and moonly
and less it shall unbe
than all the sea which only
is deeper than the sea

love is less always than to win
less never than alive
less bigger than the least begin
less littler than forgive

it is most sane and sunly
and more it cannot die
than all the sky which only
is higher than the sky

Robert Graves

SYMPTOMS OF LOVE

Love is a universal migraine,
A bright stain on the vision
Blotting out reason.

Symptoms of true love
Are leanness, jealousy,
Laggard dawns;

Are omens and nightmares—
Listening for a knock,
Waiting for a sign:

For a touch of her fingers
In a darkened room,
For a searching look.

Take courage, lover!
Can you endure such grief
At any hand but hers?

COURTSHIP

Sir John Betjeman
A SUBALTERN'S LOVE-SONG

Miss J. Hunter Dunn, Miss J. Hunter Dunn,
Furnish'd and burnish'd by Aldershot sun,
What strenuous singles we played after tea,
We in the tournament—you against me!

Love-thirty, love-forty, oh! weakness of joy,
The speed of a swallow, the grace of a boy,
With carefullest carelessness, gaily you won,
I am weak from your loveliness, Joan Hunter
    Dunn.

Miss Joan Hunter Dunn, Miss Joan Hunter
    Dunn,
How mad I am, sad I am, glad that you won.
The warm-handled racket is back in its press,
But my shock-headed victor, she loves me no less.

Her father's euonymus shines as we walk,
And swing past the summer-house, buried in talk,
And cool the verandah that welcomes us in
To the six-o'clock news and a lime-juice and gin.

The scent of the conifers, sound of the bath,
The view from my bedroom of moss-dappled
    path,
As I struggle with double-end evening tie,
For we dance at the Golf Club, my victor and I.

On the floor of her bedroom lie blazer and shorts
And the cream-coloured walls are be-trophied
    with sports,
And westering, questioning settles the sun
On your low-leaded window, Miss Joan Hunter
    Dunn.

The Hillman is waiting, the light's in the hall,
The pictures of Egypt are bright on the wall,
My sweet, I am standing beside the oak stair
And there on the landing's the light on your hair.

By roads 'not adopted', by woodlanded ways,
She drove to the club in the late summer haze,
Into nine-o'clock Camberley, heavy with bells
And mushroomy, pine-woody, evergreen smells.

Miss Joan Hunter Dunn, Miss Joan Hunter
    Dunn,
I can hear from the car-park the dance has begun.
Oh! full Surrey twilight! importunate band!
Oh! strongly adorable tennis-girl's hand!

Around us are Rovers and Austins afar,
Above us, the intimate roof of the car,
And here on my right is the girl of my choice,
With the tilt of her nose and the chime of her
    voice.

And the scent of her wrap, and the words never
    said,
And the ominous, ominous dancing ahead.
We sat in the car-park till twenty to one
And now I'm engaged to Miss Joan Hunter
    Dunn.

D. H. Lawrence

KISSES IN THE TRAIN

I saw the midlands
　Revolve through her hair;
The fields of autumn
　Stretching bare,
And sheep on the pasture
　Tossed back in a scare.

And still as ever
　The world went round,
My mouth on her pulsing
　Neck was found,
And my breast to her beating
　Breast was bound.

But my heart at the centre
　Of all, in a swound
Was still as a pivot,
　As all the ground
On its prowling orbit
　Shifted round.

And still in my nostrils
　The scent of her flesh,
And still my wet mouth
　Sought her afresh;
And still one pulse
　Through the world did thresh.

And the world all whirling
　Around in joy
Like the dance of a dervish
　Did destroy
My sense—and my reason
　Spun like a toy.

But the firm at the centre
My heart was found;
Her own to my perfect
Heart-beat bound,
Like a magnet's keeper
Closing the round.

Anon

I gently touched her hand: she gave
A look that did my soul enslave;
I pressed her rebel lips in vain;
They rose up to be pressed again.
Thus happy, I no farther meant,
Than to be pleased and innocent.

On her soft breasts my hand I laid,
And a quick, light impression made;
They with a kindly warmth did glow,
And swelled, and seemed to overflow.
Yet, trust me, I no farther meant,
Than to be pleased and innocent.

On her eyes my eyes did stay:
O'er her smooth limbs my hands did stray;
Each sense was ravished with delight,
And my soul stood prepared for flight.
Blame me not if at last I meant
More to be pleased than innocent.

W. B. Yeats
BROWN PENNY

I whispered, 'I am too young,'
And then, 'I am old enough';
Wherefore I threw a penny
To find out if I might love.
'Go and love, go and love, young man,
If the lady be young and fair.'
Ah, penny, brown penny, brown penny,
I am looped in the loops of her hair.

O love is the crooked thing,
There is nobody wise enough
To find out all that is in it,
For he would be thinking of love
Till the stars had run away
And the shadows eaten the moon.
Ah, penny, brown penny, brown penny,
One cannot begin it too soon.

Robert Browning
MEETING AT NIGHT

The grey sea and the long black land;
And the yellow half-moon large and low;
And the startled little waves that leap
In fiery ringlets from their sleep,
As I gain the cove with pushing prow,
And quench its speed i' the slushy sand.

Then a mile of warm sea-scented beach;
Three fields to cross till a farm appears;
A tap at the pane, the quick sharp scratch
And blue spurt of a lighted match,
And a voice less loud, thro' its joys and fears,
Than the two hearts beating each to each!

Sara Teasdale
THE LOOK

Strephon kissed me in the spring,
    Robin in the fall,
But Colin only looked at me
    And never kissed at all.

Strephon's kiss was lost in jest,
    Robin's lost in play,
But the kiss in Colin's eyes
    Haunts me night and day.

S. T. Coleridge
TO A LADY

'Tis not the lily brow I prize,
Nor roseate cheeks nor sunny eyes,
    Enough of lilies and of roses!
A thousand fold more dear to me
The look that gentle Love discloses,—
    That Look which Love alone can see.

Gavin Ewart

SANDRA

What bosom tapped me on the shoulder?
               Sandra.
What blooming beauty made me feel much older?
               Sandra.
What sweet Italian English made me flinch,
Then made a man of me, yes every inch?
               Sandra.

My eyes! Who dazzled them and pulled the wool
   over?
               Sandra.
Whose nippled joys were born to swell a pullover?
               Sandra.
Who lives in stereo (and I in mono)?
Who is the most beautiful Bondonno?
               Sandra.

Queen of the bus queues! Saint of the dark
   glasses!
               Sandra.
Teetering on murderous heels, aloof she passes!
               Sandra.
Sweet poison, secret, venomous as Borgias,
In young sophistication O how gorgeous!
               Sandra.

Anon

I'D HAVE YOU, QUOTH HE

I'd have you, quoth he,
Wou'd you have me, quoth she,
O where, Sir?

In my Chamber, quoth he,
In your Chamber, quoth she,
Why there, Sir?

To kiss you, quoth he,
To kiss me, quoth she,
O why, Sir?

'Cause I love it, quoth he,
Do you love it? quoth she,
So do I, Sir.

Owen Seaman

A PLEA FOR TRIGAMY

I've been trying to fashion a wifely ideal,
And find that my tastes are so far from concise
That, to marry completely, no few than three'll
                    Suffice.

I've subjected my views to severe atmospheric
Compression, but still, in defiance of force,
They distinctly fall under three heads, like a cleric
                    Discourse.

My *first* must be fashion's own fancy-bred
     daughter,
Proud, peerless, and perfect—in fact, *comme
     il faut*;
A waltzer and wit of the very first water—
                    For *show*.

But these beauties that serve to make all the men
     jealous,
Once face them alone in the family cot,
Heaven's angels incarnate (the novelists tell us)
                    They're *not*.

But so much for appearances. Now for my *second*,
My lover, the wife of my home and my heart:
Of all fortune and fate of my life to be reckon'd
                    A part.

She must know all the needs of a rational being,
Be skilled to keep council, to comfort, to coax;
And above all things else, be accomplished at seeing
                    My jokes.

I complete the ménage by including one other
With all the domestic prestige of a hen:
As my housekeeper, nurse, or it may be, a mother
                Of men.

Total *three*! and the virtues all well represented
With fewer than this such a thing can't be done;
Though I've known married men who declare
   they're contented
                With one.

Would you hunt during harvest, or hay-make in
   winter?
And how can one woman expect to combine
Certain qualifications essentially internecine?

You may say that my prospects are (legally) sunless;
I state that I find them as clear as can be:—
I will marry no wife, since I can't do with one less
              Than three.

Leigh Hunt
JENNY KISSED ME

Jenny kissed me when we met,
  Jumping from the chair she sat in;
Time, you thief! who love to get
  Sweets into your list, put that in:
Say I'm weary, say I'm sad,
  Say that health and wealth have missed me,
Say I'm growing old, but add,—
  Jenny kissed me.

Dorothy Parker
THEORY

Into love and out again,
  Thus I went, and thus I go.
Spare your voice, and hold your pen—
  Well and bitterly I know
All the songs were ever sung,
  All the words were ever said;
Could it be, when I was young,
  Some one dropped me on my head?

LOVERS

W. B. Yeats
A DRINKING SONG

Wine comes in at the mouth
And love comes in at the eye;
That's all we know for truth
Before we grow old and die.
I lift the glass to my mouth,
I look at you, and I sigh.

Anonymous
MADRIGAL

My love in her attire doth show her wit,
　　It does so well become her;
For every season she hath dressings fit,
　　For Winter, Spring, and Summer.
　　No beauty she doth miss
　　When all her robes are on:
　　But Beauty's self she is
　　When all her robes are gone.

Anonymous

THERE IS A LADY

There is a Lady sweet and kind,
Was never face so pleased my mind;
I did but see her passing by,
And yet I love her till I die.

Her gesture, motion, and her smiles,
Her wit, her voice my heart beguiles,
Beguiles my heart, I know not why,
And yet I love her till I die.

Cupid is winged and doth range,
Her country so my love doth change:
But change she earth, or change she sky,
Yet will I love her till I die.

Ogden Nash

ALWAYS MARRY AN APRIL GIRL

Praise the spells and bless the charms,
I found April in my arms.
April golden, April cloudy.
Gracious, cruel, tender, rowdy;
April soft in flowered languor,
April cold with sudden anger,
Ever changing, ever true—
I love April. I love you.

W. H. Auden
LULLABY

Lay your sleeping head, my love,
Human on my faithless arm;
Time and fevers burn away
Individual beauty from
Thoughtful children, and the grave
Proves the child ephemeral:
But in my arms till break of day
Let the living creature lie,
Mortal, guilty, but to me
The entirely beautiful.

Soul and body have no bounds:
To lovers as they lie upon
Her tolerant enchanted slope
In their ordinary swoon,
Grave the vision Venus sends
Of supernatural sympathy,
Universal love and hope:
While an abstract insight wakes
Among the glaciers and the rocks
The hermit's carnal ecstasy.

Certainty, fidelity
On the stroke of midnight pass
Like vibrations of a bell,
And fashionable madmen raise
Their pedantic boring cry;
Every farthing of the cost,
All the dreaded cards foretell,
Shall be paid, but from this night
Not a whisper, not a thought,
Not a kiss nor look be lost.

37

Beauty, midnight, vision dies:
Let the winds of dawn that blow
Softly round your dreaming head
Such a day of sweetness show
Eye and knocking heart may bless,
Find the mortal world enough;
Noons of dryness find you fed
By the involuntary powers,
Nights of insult let you pass
Watched by every human love.

Stephen Spender
DAYBREAK

At dawn she lay with her profile at that angle
Which, when she sleeps, seems the carved face of
   an angel.
Her hair a harp, the hand of a breeze follows
And plays, against the white cloud of the pillows.
Then, in a flush of rose, she woke, and her eyes that
   opened
Swam in blue through her rose flesh that dawned.
From her dew of lips, the drop of one word
Fell like the first of fountains: murmured
'Darling', upon my ears the song of the first bird.
'My dream becomes my dream,' she said, 'come
   true.
I waken from you to my dream of you.'
Oh, my own wakened dream then dared assume
The audacity of her sleep. Our dreams
Poured into each other's arms, like streams.

Paul Ramsey

HE, THEN

No, she said. Please, she said.
He tasted her hunger, his fingers
touching her ear lobe, the flesh behind it.
None the less, he did not kiss her.
In the hallway and down the stairs he trembled
with the hurt of his leaving.
In the raw snow blowing in the wind,
in the slide of the water loosing,
he said, Please, he said Please, in the snow.

Alan Ross

AFTER LOVE

After love, to continue the caress
Is both to insure
Against sadness and to reassure
The one and the other that "Yes"
Has not become "No,"
And the urge to get up and dress,
Leave a kiss on the brow, and go,
Is one that will subside
In the slowly returning tide
That brings to the next caress
True elements of tenderness.

Charles Webbe
AGAINST INDIFFERENCE

More love or more disdain I crave:
   Sweet, be not still indifferent:
O send me quickly to my grave,
   Or else afford me more content!
Or love or hate me more or less,
For love abhors all lukewarmness.

Give me a tempest if 'twill drive
   Me to the place where I would be;
Or if you'll have me still alive,
   Confess you will be kind to me.
Give hopes of bliss or dig my grave:
More love or more disdain I crave.

Robert Browning
A WOMAN'S LAST WORD

Let's contend no more, Love,
Strive nor weep:
All be as before, Love,
—Only sleep!

What so wild as words are?
I and thou
In debate, as birds are,
Hawk on bough!

See the creature stalking
While we speak!
Hush and hide the talking,
Cheek on cheek!

What so false as truth is,
False to thee?
Where the serpent's tooth is
Shun the tree—

Where the apple reddens
Never pry—
Lest we lose our Edens,
Eve and I.

Be a god and hold me
With a charm!
Be a man and fold me
With thine arm!

Teach me, only teach, Love!
As I ought
I will speak thy speech, Love,
Think thy thought—

Meet, if thou require it,
Both demands,
Laying flesh and spirit
In thy hands.

That shall be tomorrow
Not to-night:
I must bury sorrow
Out of sight:

—Must a little weep, Love,
(Foolish me!)
And so fall asleep, Love,
Loved by thee.

W. R. Rodgers
THE LOVERS

After the tiff there was silence, till
One word, flung in centre like single stone,
Starred and cracked the ice of her resentment
To its edge. From that stung core opened and
Poured up one outward and widening wave
Of eager and extravagant anger.

Francis William Bourdillon
NIGHT

The night has a thousand eyes,
   And the day but one;
Yet the light of the bright world dies
   With the dying sun.

The mind has a thousand eyes,
   And the heart but one;
Yet the light of a whole life dies,
   When love is done.

P. G. *Wodehouse*

THE GOURMET'S LOVE-SONG

How strange is love; I am not one
Who Cupid's power belittles,
For Cupid 'tis who makes me shun
My customary victuals.
Oh, EFFIE, since that painful scene
That left me broken-hearted,
My appetite, erstwhile so keen,
Has utterly departed.

My form, my friends observe with pain,
Is growing daily thinner.
Love only occupies the brain
That once could think of dinner.
Around me myriad waiters flit,
With meat and drink to ply men;
Alone, disconsolate, I sit,
And feed on thoughts of Hymen.

The kindly waiters hear my groan,
They strive to charm with curry;
They tempt me with a devilled bone—
I beg them not to worry.
Soup, whitebait, entrées, fricassees,
They bring me uninvited.
I need them not, for what are these
To one whose life is blighted?

They show me dishes rich and rare,
But ah! my pulse no joy stirs.
For savouries I've ceased to care,
I hate the thought of oysters.
They bring me roast, they bring me boiled,
But all in vain they woo me;
The waiters softly mutter, 'Foiled!'
The chef, poor man, looks gloomy.

So, EFFIE, turn that shell-like ear,
Nor to my sighing close it,
You cannot doubt that I'm sincere—
This ballad surely shows it.
No longer spurn the suit I press,
Respect my agitation,
Do change your mind, and answer, 'Yes',
And save me from starvation.

Samuel Hoffenstein

Lovely lady, who does so
All my waking haunt,
Tell me, tell me, do you know
What the hell you want?

Lady, to whose feet I'd bring
The world, if I could win it,
Are you sure of anything
For a single minute?

You whose eyes can kindle flame
Only Death could smother,
Tell me, please, does any dame
Differ from another?

Was the apple applesauce
Eve ate in the garden?
Aren't you all a total loss?
No? I beg your pardon!

Bhatrhari

In former days we'd both agree
That you were me, and I was you.
What has now happened to us two,
That you are you, and I am me?

She who is always in my thoughts prefers
Another man, and does not think of me.
Yet he seeks for another's love, not hers;
And some poor girl is grieving for my sake.
   Why then, the devil take
Both her and him; and love; and her; and
   me.

Translated from the Sanskrit by John Brough

Mathew Prior
A LOVER'S ANGER

A Chloé came into the room t'other day,
I peevish began: Where so long could you stay?
In your lifetime you never regarded your hour:
You promised at two: and (pray look, child)
   'tis four.
A lady's watch needs neither figures nor wheels:
'Tis enough, that 'tis loaded with baubles and seals.
A temper so heedless no mortal can bear—
Thus far I went on with a resolute air.
Lord bless me! said she; let a body but speak:
Here's an ugly hard rosebud fall'n into my neck:
It has hurt me, and vexed me to such a degree—
See here; for you never believe me; pray see,
On the left side my breast what a mark it has made,
So saying, her bosom she careless displayed.
That seat of delight I with wonder surveyed;
And forgot every word I designed to have said.

William Walsh

THE DESPAIRING LOVER

Distracted with care,
For Phyllis the fair;
Since nothing could move her,
Poor Damon, her lover,
Resolves in despair
No longer to languish,
Nor bear so much anguish;
But, mad with his love,
To a precipice goes;
Where, a leap from above
Would soon finish his woes.
When in rage he came there,
Beholding how steep
The sides did appear,
And the bottom how deep;
His torments projecting,
And sadly reflecting,
That a lover forsaken
A new love may get;
But a neck, when once broken,
Can never be set:
And, that he could die
Whenever he would;
But that he could live
But as long as he could;
How grievous soever
The torment might grow,
He scorned to endeavour
To finish it so.
But bold, unconcerned
At the thoughts of the pain,
He calmly returned
To his cottage again.

John Dryden
From *THE SPANISH FRIAR*

Farewell ungrateful traitor,
　　Farewell my perjured swain,
Let never injured creature
　　Believe a man again.
The pleasure of possessing
Surpasses all expressing,
But 'tis too short a blessing,
　　And love too long a pain.

'Tis easy to deceive us
　　In pity of your pain,
But when we love you leave us
　　To rail at you in vain.
Before we have descried it,
There is no bliss beside it,
But she that once has tried it
　　Will never love again.

The passion you pretended
　　Was only to obtain,
But when the charm is ended
　　The charmer you disdain.
Your love by ours we measure
Till we have lost our treasure,
But dying is a pleasure,
　　When living is a pain.

Lord Byron

WE'LL GO NO MORE A-ROVING

So, we'll go no more a-roving
   So late into the night,
Though the heart be still as loving,
   And the moon be still as bright.

For the sword outwears its sheath,
   And the soul wears out the breast,
And the heart must pause to breathe,
   And love itself have rest.

Though the night was made for loving,
   And the day returns too soon,
Yet we'll go no more a-roving
   By the light of the moon.

Walter Savage Landor

SEPARATION

There is a mountain and a wood between us,
Where the lone shepherd and late bird have seen us
   Morning and noon and eventide repass.
Between us now the mountain and the wood
Seem standing darker than last year they stood,
   And say we must not cross—alas! alas!

King Henry VIII to Anne Boleyn

[1528]

My mistress and friend,

I and my heart put ourselves in your hands, begging you to recommend us to your good grace and not to let absence lessen your affection, for it were great pity to increase their pain, seeing that absence does that sufficiently and more than I could ever have thought possible; reminding us of a point in astronomy, which is that the longer the days are the farther off is the sun and yet the hotter; so is it with our love, for although by absence we are parted it nevertheless keeps its fervency, at least in my case and hoping the like of yours; assuring you that for myself the pang of absence is already too great, and when I think of the increase of what I must needs suffer it would be well nigh intolerable but for my firm hope of your unchangeable affection; and sometimes to put you in mind of this, and seeing that in person I cannot be with you, I send you now something most nearly pertaining thereto that is at present possible to send, that is to say, my picture set in a bracelet with the whole device which you already know; wishing myself in their place when it shall please you. This by the hand of

> Your loyal servant and friend,
> H Rex

OTHER
KINDS
OF
LOVE

Viscount Grey of Fallodon

Generally speaking, it seems at least probable that swans, geese, sheldrakes and those kinds of waterfowl in which the plumage of the male and female is the same throughout the year . . . pair for life in a wild state. In all these species there is probably no separation of the male from the female during the rearing of the young, and when this is so, there is no reason why the mating should not be permanent.

Birds that remain in pairs throughout the year are distressed if they are separated at any season, and to anyone who observes this and who watches them together, it is apparent that even in autumn and winter the mated birds have positive enjoyment in each other's society. . . .

William E. Henley
THE BLACKBIRD

The nightingale has a lyre of gold,
 The lark's is a clarion call,
And the blackbird plays but a boxwood flute,
 But I love him best of all.

For his song is all of the joy of life,
 And we in the mad, spring weather,
We two have listened till he sang
 Our hearts and lips together.

Ogden Nash
THE CUCKOO

Cuckoos lead Bohemian lives,
They fail as husbands and as wives,
Therefore they cynically disparage
Everybody else's marriage.

Turgenev
THE SPARROW

I was returning from hunting, and walking along an avenue of the garden, my dog running in front of me.

Suddenly he took shorter steps, and began to steal along as though tracking game.

I looked along the avenue, and saw a young sparrow, with yellow about its beak and down on its head. It had fallen out of the nest (the wind was violently shaking the birch-trees in the avenue) and sat unable to move, helplessly flapping its half-grown wings.

My dog was slowly approaching it, when, suddenly darting down from a tree close by, an old dark-throated sparrow fell like a stone right before his nose, and all ruffled up, terrified, with despairing and pitiful cheeps, it flung itself twice towards the open jaws of shining teeth.

It sprang to save; it cast itself before its nestling . . . but all its tiny body was shaking with terror; its note was harsh and strange. Swooning with fear, it offered itself up!

What a huge monster must the dog have seemed to it! And yet it could not stay on its high branch out of danger. . . . A force stronger than its will flung it down.

My Trésor stood still, drew back. . . . Clearly he too recognised this force.

I hastened to call off the disconcerted dog, and went away, full of reverence.

Yes; do not laugh. I felt reverence for that tiny heroic bird, for its impulse of love.

Love, I thought, is stronger than death or the fear of death. Only by it, by love, life holds together and advances.

W. H. Davies
THE KINGFISHER

It was the Rainbow gave thee birth,
   And left thee all her lovely hues;
And, as her mother's name was Tears,
   So runs it in thy blood to choose
For haunts the lonely pools, and keep
In company with trees that weep.

Go you and, with such glorious hues,
   Live with proud Peacocks in green parks;
On lawns as smooth as shining glass,
   Let every feather show its marks;
Get thee on boughs and clap thy wings
Before the windows of proud kings.

Nay, lovely Bird, thou art not vain;
   Thou hast no proud ambitious mind;
I also love a quiet place
   That's green, away from all mankind;
A lonely pool, and let a tree
Sigh with her bosom over me.

Robert Bridges
THE LINNET

I heard a linnet courting
　　His lady in the spring:
His mates were idly sporting,
　　Nor stayed to hear him sing
　　　　His song of love.—
I fear my speech distorting
　　　　His tender love.

The phrases of his pleading
　　Were full of young delight;
And she that gave him heeding
　　Interpreted aright
　　　　His gay, sweet notes,—
So sadly marred in the reading,—
　　　　His tender notes.

And when he ceased, the hearer
　　Awaited the refrain,
Till swiftly perching nearer
　　He sang his song again,
　　　　His pretty song:—
Would that my verse spake clearer
　　　　His tender song!

Ye happy, airy creatures!
　　That in the merry spring
Think not of what misfeatures
　　Or cares the year may bring;
　　　　But unto love
Resign your simple natures
　　　　To tender love.

Henri Fabré

With a view to mating, the sole end of its life, the great moth—(the Great Peacock)—is endowed with a marvellous prerogative. It has the power to discover the object of its desire in spite of distance, in spite of obstacles. A few hours, for two or three nights, are given to its search, its nuptial flights. If it cannot profit by them, all is ended; the compass fails, the lamp expires.

The Great Peacock renounces the joys of the palate; but with them it surrenders long life. Two or three nights—just long enough to allow the couple to meet and mate—and all is over; the great butterfly is dead. . . .

Ogden Nash

THE OYSTER

The oyster's a confusing suitor:
It's masc., and fem., and even neuter.
But whether husband, pal or wife
It leads a painless sort of life.
I'd like to be an oyster, say,
In August, June, July or May.

THE SHRIMP

A shrimp who sought his lady shrimp
Could catch no glimpse,
Not even a glimp.
At times, translucence
Is rather a nuisance.

THE TURTLE

The turtle lives twixt plated decks
Which practically conceal its sex.
I think it clever of the turtle
In such a fix to be so fertile.

DEVOTION

Ogden Nash

THE TROUBLE WITH WOMEN IS MEN

A husband is a man who two minutes after his
  head touches the pillow is snoring like an
  overloaded omnibus,
Particularly on those occasions when between the
  humidity and the mosquitoes your own bed is
  no longer a bed, but an insomnibus,
And if you turn on the light for a little reading he
  is sensitive to the faintest gleam,
But if by any chance you are asleep and he
  wakeful, he is not slow to rouse you with the
  complaint that he can't close his eyes, what
  about slipping downstairs and freezing him a
  cooling dish of pistachio ice cream.
His touch with a bottle opener is sure,
But he cannot help you get a tight dress over your
  head without catching three hooks and a button
  in your coiffure.
Nor can he so much as wash his ears without
  leaving an inch of water on the bathroom
  linoleum,
But if you mention it you evoke not a promise to
  splash no more but a mood of deep
  melancholium.
Indeed, each time he transgresses your chance of
  correcting his faults grows lesser,
Because he produces either a maddeningly logical
  explanation or a look of martyrdom which
  leaves you instead of him feeling the remorse of
  the transgressor.
Such are husbandly foibles, but there are
  moments when a foible ceases to be a foible.

Next time you ask for a glass of water and when
he brings it you have a needle almost threaded
and instead of setting it down he stands there
holding it out to you, just kick him fairly hard
in the stomach, you will find it thoroughly
enjoible.

Robert Graves

A SLICE OF WEDDING CAKE

Why have such scores of lovely, gifted girls
    Married impossible men?
Simple self-sacrifice may be ruled out,
    And missionary endeavour, nine times out of
    ten.

Repeat 'impossible men': not merely rustic,
    Foul-tempered or depraved
(Dramatic foils chosen to show the world
    How well women behave, and always have
    behaved).

Impossible men: idle, illiterate,
    Self-pitying, dirty, sly,
For whose appearance even in City parks
    Excuses must be made to casual passers-by.

Has God's supply of tolerable husbands
    Fallen, in fact, so low?
Or do I always over-value woman
    At the expense of man?
                        Do I?
                            It might be so.

William Shakespeare

Shall I compare thee to a summer's day?
   Thou art more lovely and more temperate:
Rough winds do shake the darling buds of May,
   And summer's lease hath all too short a date:
Sometime too hot the eye of heaven shines,
   And often is his gold complexion dimmed;
And every fair from fair sometime declines,
   By chance, or nature's changing course
untrimmed;

But thy eternal summer shall not fade,
   Nor lose possession of that fair thou owest,
Nor shall death brag thou wanderest in his shade,
   When in eternal lines to time thou growest;
So long as men can breathe, or eyes can see,
So long lives this, and this gives life to thee.

W. B. Yeats

THE PITY OF LOVE

A pity beyond all telling
Is hid in the heart of love:
The folk who are buying and selling,
The clouds on their journey above,
The cold wet winds ever blowing,
And the shadowy hazel grove
Where mouse-grey waters are flowing,
Threaten the head that I love.

Sara Teasdale

GIFTS

I gave my first love laughter,
    I gave my second tears,
I gave my third love silence
    Through all the years.

My first love gave me singing,
    My second eyes to see,
But oh, it was my third love
    Who gave my soul to me.

Ogden Nash

TO MY VALENTINE

More than a catbird hates a cat,
Or a criminal hates a clue,
Or the Axis hates the United States,
That's how much I love you.

I love you more than a duck can swim,
And more than a grapefruit squirts,
I love you more than gin rummy is a bore,
And more than a toothache hurts.

As a shipwrecked sailor hates the sea,
Or a juggler hates a shove,
As a hostess detests unexpected guests,
That's how much you I love.

I love you more than a wasp can sting,
And more than the subway jerks,
I love you as much as a beggar needs a crutch,
And more than a hangnail irks.

I swear to you by the stars above,
And below, if such there be,
As the High Court loathes perjurious oaths,
That's how you're loved by me.

Samuel Hoffenstein

My mate, my friend, my love, my life,
My bosom's—as the phrase is—wife;
My comrade in the hour of woe—
An hour whose limits I don't know—
My star in darkness, solace, balm,
My prophylaxis, refuge, calm,
Companion of the million blights
That plague my liver, purse and lights;
My pleasant garden in the gloam,
My all—if you were ever home!

T. S. Eliot

A DEDICATION TO MY WIFE

To whom I owe the leaping delight
That quickens my senses in our wakingtime
And the rhythm that governs the repose of our
    sleepingtime,
    The breathing in unison

Of lovers whose bodies smell of each other
Who think the same thoughts without need of
    speech
And babble the same speech without need of
    meaning.

No peevish winter wind shall chill
No sullen tropic sun shall wither
The roses in the rose-garden which is ours and ours
    only

But this dedication is for others to read:
These are private words addressed to you in public.

Robert Graves

SHE TELLS HER LOVE
WHILE HALF ASLEEP

She tells her love while half asleep,
  In the dark hours,
    With half-words whispered low:
As Earth stirs in her winter sleep
  And puts out grass and flowers
    Despite the snow,
    Despite the falling snow.

Donald Davie
TIME PASSING, BELOVED

Time passing, and the memories of love
Coming back to me, carissima, no more
   mockingly
Than ever before, time passing, unslackening,
Unhastening, steadily; and no more
Bitterly, beloved, the memories of love
Coming into the shore.

How will it end? Time passing, and our passages
   of love
As ever, beloved, blind
As ever before; time binding, unbinding
About us; and yet to remember
Never less chastening, nor the flame of love
Less like an ember.

What will become of us? Time
Passing, beloved, and we in a sealed
Assurance unassailed
By memory. How can it end,
This siege of a shore that no misgivings
   have steeled,
No doubts defend?

Elizabeth Barrett Browning

SONNET XLIII
FROM THE PORTUGUESE

How do I love thee? Let me count the ways.
I love thee to the depth and breadth and height
My soul can reach, when feeling out of sight
For the ends of Being and Ideal Grace.
I love thee to the level of every day's
Most quiet need, by sun and candlelight.
I love thee freely, as men strive for Right;
I love thee purely, as they turn from Praise.
I love thee with the passion put to use
In my old griefs, and with my childhood's faith.
I love thee with a love I seemed to lose
With my lost saints,—I love thee with the breath,
Smiles, tears, of all my life!—and, if God choose,
I shall but love thee better after death.

Yeats

WHEN YOU ARE OLD

When you are old and grey and full of sleep,
And nodding by the fire, take down this book,
And slowly read, and dream of the soft look
Your eyes had once, and of their shadows deep;

How many loved your moments of glad grace,
And loved your beauty with love false or true,
But one man loved the pilgrim soul in you,
And loved the sorrows of your changing face;

And bending down beside the glowing bars,
Murmur, a little sadly, how Love fled
And paced upon the mountains overhead
And hid his face amid a crowd of stars.

Acknowledgements

The publisher would like to express gratitude to the following for their permission to include in this volume copyright poems and passages:

Jonathan Cape Ltd. and the Executors of the Estate of W.H. Davies for 'The Kingfisher' by W.H. Davies from *The Complete Poems of W.H. Davies*; Paul Ramsey for 'He Then' by Paul Ramsey which first appeared in *Epoch* in 1968; Gerald Duckworth & Co. Ltd. for 'Theory' by Dorothy Parker from *The Collected Dorothy Parker*; Mr Gavin Ewart for his poem 'Sandra'; Eyre & Spottiswoode (Publishers) Ltd. for 'After Love' by Alan Ross from *Alan Ross Poems 1942–67*; Faber and Faber Ltd. for 'Lay Your Sleeping Head' by W.H. Auden from *Collected Shorter Poems 1927–1957 by W.H. Auden*; Faber and Faber Ltd. for 'A Dedication To My Wife' from *Collected Poems 1909–1926 by T.S. Eliot*; Faber and Faber Ltd. for 'Daybreak' from *Collected Poems by Stephen Spender*; Robert Graves for 'She Tells Her Love While Half Asleep', 'Symptoms of Love', 'A Slice of Wedding Cake' by Robert Graves from *The Collected Poems of Robert Graves*; Macmillan Publishing Co. Inc. for 'The Look' and 'Gifts' from *Collected Poems of Sara Teasdale* 1915, renewed in 1943 by Mamie T. Wheless; Liveright Publishing Corporation, New York for extracts from *A Treasury of Humorous Verse* by Samuel Hoffenstein 1946, renewed 1974 by Liveright Publishing Corporation; John Murray Ltd. for 'A Subaltern's Love-Song' by Sir John Betjeman from *Collected Poems by John Betjeman*; the Estate of Ogden Nash for 'Always Marry an April Girl', 'The Oyster', 'The Turtle', 'The Cuckoo', 'The Trouble With Women Is Men', 'To My Valentine', 'The Shrimp' by Ogden Nash from *The Collected Poems of Ogden Nash*; Oxford University

Press for 'The Linnet' from *The Poetical Works of Robert Bridges*; Laurence Pollinger Ltd. and the Estate of the late Mrs Frieda Lawrence Ravagli for 'Kisses in the Train' by D.H. Lawrence from *The Complete Poems of D.H. Lawrence* published by William Heinemann Ltd; Routledge & Kegan Paul Ltd. for 'Time Passing Beloved' by Donald Davie from *A Winter Talent*; the Estate of P.G. Wodehouse for 'The Gourmet's Love-Song by P.G. Wodehouse from *Punch* 1901; M.B. Yeats and Macmillan & Co. for 'Brown Penny', 'The Pity of Love', 'A Drinking Song', 'When you are Old' by W.B. Yeats from *The Collected Poems of W.B. Yeats*.